THIS PLANNER BELONGS TO

_____

School _____

Grade _____ Room _____

Address _____

_____

Email _____

Phone _____

CONTACTS and volunteers

Name

Contact Info

WELCOME

Schedule

SCHOOL BEGINS: _____

LUNCH: _____   RECESS: _____

SPECIALS: _____

SCHOOL ENDS: _____

Need help?

RELIABLE STUDENTS: _____

TEACHERS: _____

PRINCIPAL: _____

VICE PRINCIPAL: _____

OTHER STAFF: _____

Special Schedules

NAME	TIME / LOCATION

Additional Notes

_____

_____

_____

_____

_____

Communication Log

DATE	TYPE	NAME	PURPOSE	NOTES
	📱 @ 📋 👥			
	📱 @ 📋 👥			
	📱 @ 📋 👥			
	📱 @ 📋 👥			
	📱 @ 📋 👥			
	📱 @ 📋 👥			
	📱 @ 📋 👥			
	📱 @ 📋 👥			
	📱 @ 📋 👥			
	📱 @ 📋 👥			
	📱 @ 📋 👥			
	📱 @ 📋 👥			
	📱 @ 📋 👥			
	📱 @ 📋 👥			
	📱 @ 📋 👥			
	📱 @ 📋 👥			
	📱 @ 📋 👥			
	📱 @ 📋 👥			
	📱 @ 📋 👥			
	📱 @ 📋 👥			
	📱 @ 📋 👥			
	📱 @ 📋 👥			
	📱 @ 📋 👥			
	📱 @ 📋 👥			
	📱 @ 📋 👥			

Communication Log

DATE	TYPE	NAME	PURPOSE	NOTES
	📱 @ 📋 👥			
	📱 @ 📋 👥			
	📱 @ 📋 👥			
	📱 @ 📋 👥			
	📱 @ 📋 👥			
	📱 @ 📋 👥			
	📱 @ 📋 👥			
	📱 @ 📋 👥			
	📱 @ 📋 👥			
	📱 @ 📋 👥			
	📱 @ 📋 👥			
	📱 @ 📋 👥			
	📱 @ 📋 👥			
	📱 @ 📋 👥			
	📱 @ 📋 👥			
	📱 @ 📋 👥			
	📱 @ 📋 👥			
	📱 @ 📋 👥			
	📱 @ 📋 👥			
	📱 @ 📋 👥			
	📱 @ 📋 👥			
	📱 @ 📋 👥			
	📱 @ 📋 👥			
	📱 @ 📋 👥			
	📱 @ 📋 👥			
	📱 @ 📋 👥			
	📱 @ 📋 👥			

news and Notes

News and Notes

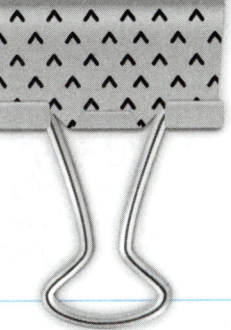

PLAN IT

Use these pages to create a classroom plan, record seating charts, create checklists, sketch plans, etc. The options are endless!

PLAN IT

Use these pages to create a classroom plan, record seating charts, create checklists, sketch plans, etc. The options are endless!

YEAR at a glance

JULY

AUGUST

SEPTEMBER

OCTOBER

NOVEMBER

DECEMBER

YEAR at a glance

JANUARY

FEBRUARY

MARCH

APRIL

MAY

JUNE

JULY

SUNDAY	MONDAY	TUESDAY	WEDNESDAY

Important Dates

_____
_____
_____

Goals

_____
_____
_____

THURSDAY	FRIDAY	SATURDAY
○	○	○
○	○	○
○	○	○
○	○	○
○	○	○

Have To Do

○ _____
○ _____
○ _____
○ _____
○ _____
○ _____
○ _____
○ _____
○ _____
○ _____
○ _____

Notes

_____
_____
_____
_____
_____
_____
_____
_____
_____
_____

PSST! USE THESE GUIDES TO KEEP YOUR TABS PERFECTLY PLACED.

AUGUST

Dream Big

SUNDAY	MONDAY	TUESDAY	WEDNESDAY

Important Dates

_____

_____

_____

Goals

_____

_____

_____

THURSDAY	FRIDAY	SATURDAY
◯	◯	◯
◯	◯	◯
◯	◯	◯
◯	◯	◯
◯	◯	◯

Have To Do

- ◯ _____
- ◯ _____
- ◯ _____
- ◯ _____
- ◯ _____
- ◯ _____
- ◯ _____
- ◯ _____
- ◯ _____
- ◯ _____
- ◯ _____
- ◯ _____

Notes

_____

_____

_____

_____

_____

_____

_____

_____

_____

_____

_____

SEPTEMBER

SUNDAY	MONDAY	TUESDAY	WEDNESDAY

Important Dates

_____
_____
_____

Goals

_____
_____
_____

THURSDAY	FRIDAY	SATURDAY
○	○	○
○	○	○
○	○	○
○	○	○
○	○	○

Have To Do

○ _____
○ _____
○ _____
○ _____
○ _____
○ _____
○ _____
○ _____
○ _____
○ _____
○ _____
○ _____

Notes

_____
_____
_____
_____
_____
_____
_____
_____
_____
_____
_____
_____
_____

OCTOBER

SUNDAY	MONDAY	TUESDAY	WEDNESDAY

Important Dates

_____
_____
_____

Goals

_____
_____
_____

THURSDAY	FRIDAY	SATURDAY

Have To Do

○ _____
○ _____
○ _____
○ _____
○ _____
○ _____
○ _____
○ _____
○ _____
○ _____
○ _____
○ _____

Notes

_____
_____
_____
_____
_____
_____
_____
_____
_____
_____
_____

NOVEMBER

SUNDAY	MONDAY	TUESDAY	WEDNESDAY

Important Dates

_____

_____

_____

Goals

_____

_____

_____

THURSDAY	FRIDAY	SATURDAY
○	○	○
○	○	○
○	○	○
○	○	○
○	○	○

Have To Do

○ _____
○ _____
○ _____
○ _____
○ _____
○ _____
○ _____
○ _____
○ _____
○ _____

Notes

_____
_____
_____
_____
_____
_____
_____
_____
_____
_____
_____

DECEMBER

SUNDAY	MONDAY	TUESDAY	WEDNESDAY

Important Dates

_____
_____
_____

Goals

_____
_____

THURSDAY	FRIDAY	SATURDAY
◯	◯	◯
◯	◯	◯
◯	◯	◯
◯	◯	◯
◯	◯	◯

Have To Do

- ◯ _____
- ◯ _____
- ◯ _____
- ◯ _____
- ◯ _____
- ◯ _____
- ◯ _____
- ◯ _____
- ◯ _____
- ◯ _____
- ◯ _____

Notes

_____
_____
_____
_____
_____
_____
_____
_____
_____
_____
_____
_____
_____

JANUARY

SUNDAY	MONDAY	TUESDAY	WEDNESDAY

Important Dates

_____
_____
_____

Goals

_____
_____

THURSDAY	FRIDAY	SATURDAY
○	○	○
○	○	○
○	○	○
○	○	○
○	○	○

Have To Do

○ _____
○ _____
○ _____
○ _____
○ _____
○ _____
○ _____
○ _____
○ _____
○ _____
○ _____

Notes

_____
_____
_____
_____
_____
_____
_____
_____
_____
_____
_____
_____

FEBRUARY

SUNDAY	MONDAY	TUESDAY	WEDNESDAY

_____
_____
_____

_____
_____

THURSDAY	FRIDAY	SATURDAY
○	○	○
○	○	○
○	○	○
○	○	○
○	○	○

Have To Do

○ _____
○ _____
○ _____
○ _____
○ _____
○ _____
○ _____
○ _____
○ _____
○ _____
○ _____

Notes

_____
_____
_____
_____
_____
_____
_____
_____
_____
_____
_____
_____
_____
_____

MARCH

Smile Often

SUNDAY	MONDAY	TUESDAY	WEDNESDAY

Goals

THURSDAY	FRIDAY	SATURDAY	Have To Do
○	○	○	○
			○
			○
			○
○	○	○	○
			○
			○
			○
			○
○	○	○	○
			○
			○
○	○	○	Notes
○	○	○	

 # APRIL

Shine Bright

SUNDAY	MONDAY	TUESDAY	WEDNESDAY

Important Dates

_____

_____

_____

Goals

_____

_____

_____

THURSDAY	FRIDAY	SATURDAY
◯	◯	◯
◯	◯	◯
◯	◯	◯
◯	◯	◯
◯	◯	◯

Have To Do

◯ _____
◯ _____
◯ _____
◯ _____
◯ _____
◯ _____
◯ _____
◯ _____
◯ _____
◯ _____
◯ _____

Notes

_____
_____
_____
_____
_____
_____
_____
_____
_____
_____
_____
_____
_____
_____

MAY

Believe in Yourself

SUNDAY	MONDAY	TUESDAY	WEDNESDAY
○	○	○	○
○	○	○	○
○	○	○	○
○	○	○	○
○	○	○	○

THURSDAY	FRIDAY	SATURDAY
○	○	○
○	○	○
○	○	○
○	○	○
○	○	○

Have To Do

○ _____
○ _____
○ _____
○ _____
○ _____
○ _____
○ _____
○ _____
○ _____
○ _____
○ _____

Notes

JUNE

Yes! You can

SUNDAY	MONDAY	TUESDAY	WEDNESDAY
◯	◯	◯	◯
◯	◯	◯	◯
◯	◯	◯	◯
◯	◯	◯	◯
◯	◯	◯	◯

Important Dates

_____
_____
_____

Goals

_____
_____
_____

THURSDAY	FRIDAY	SATURDAY
◯	◯	◯
◯	◯	◯
◯	◯	◯
◯	◯	◯
◯	◯	◯

Have To Do

○ _____
○ _____
○ _____
○ _____
○ _____
○ _____
○ _____
○ _____
○ _____
○ _____
○ _____
○ _____

Notes

_____
_____
_____
_____
_____
_____
_____
_____
_____
_____
_____
_____
_____

WEEK

subject	subject	subject

MON. /

TUES. /

WED. /

THURS. /

FRI. /

subject	subject	subject	subject

PSST! CUT THIS CORNER OFF EACH WEEK TO MARK AND FIND YOUR PLACE EASILY.

WEEK

subject	subject	subject

MON.
/

TUES.
/

WED.
/

THURS.
/

FRI.
/

subject	subject	subject	subject

WEEK

subject	subject	subject

MON. /

TUES. /

WED. /

THURS. /

FRI. /

subject	subject	subject	subject

WEEK

subject	subject	subject

MON. /

TUES. /

WED. /

THURS. /

FRI. /

subject	subject	subject	subject

WEEK

Subject	Subject	Subject

MON.
/

TUES.
/

WED.
/

THURS.
/

FRI.
/

subject	subject	subject	subject

WEEK #	subject	subject	subject
MON. /			
TUES. /			
WED. /			
THURS. /			
FRI. /			

subject	subject	subject	subject

WEEK

subject	subject	subject

MON.
/

TUES.
/

WED.
/

THURS.
/

FRI.
/

subject	subject	subject	subject

WEEK

subject	subject	subject

MON.
/

TUES.
/

WED.
/

THURS.
/

FRI.
/

subject	subject	subject	subject

WEEK

subject	subject	subject

MON.
/

TUES.
/

WED.
/

THURS.
/

FRI.
/

subject	subject	subject	subject

WEEK

subject	subject	subject

MON. /

TUES. /

WED. /

THURS. /

FRI. /

subject	subject	subject	subject

WEEK

subject	subject	subject

MON.
/

TUES.
/

WED.
/

THURS.
/

FRI.
/

subject	subject	subject	subject

WEEK

subject	subject	subject

MON.
/

TUES.
/

WED.
/

THURS.
/

FRI.
/

subject	subject	subject	subject

WEEK

subject	subject	subject

MON. /

TUES. /

WED. /

THURS. /

FRI. /

subject	subject	subject	subject

WEEK

subject	subject	subject

MON.
/

TUES.
/

WED.
/

THURS.
/

FRI.
/

subject	subject	subject	subject

WEEK

subject	subject	subject

MON. /

TUES. /

WED. /

THURS. /

FRI. /

subject	subject	subject	subject

WEEK

subject	subject	subject

MON.
/

TUES.
/

WED.
/

THURS.
/

FRI.
/

subject	subject	subject	subject

WEEK

subject	subject	subject

MON.
/

TUES.
/

WED.
/

THURS.
/

FRI.
/

subject	subject	subject	subject

WEEK#

subject	subject	subject

MON.
/

TUES.
/

WED.
/

THURS.
/

FRI.
/

subject	subject	subject	subject

WEEK

subject	subject	subject

MON.
/

TUES.
/

WED.
/

THURS.
/

FRI.
/

subject	subject	subject

subject	subject	subject	subject

WEEK

subject	subject	subject

MON.
/

TUES.
/

WED.
/

THURS.
/

FRI.
/

74

subject	subject	subject	subject

WEEK#

subject	subject	subject

MON.
/

TUES.
/

WED.
/

THURS.
/

FRI.
/

subject	subject	subject

subject	subject	subject	subject

WEEK

subject	subject	subject

MON.
/

TUES.
/

WED.
/

THURS.
/

FRI.
/

subject	subject	subject	subject

WEEK

subject	subject	subject

MON. /

TUES. /

WED. /

THURS. /

FRI. /

subject	subject	subject	subject

WEEK

subject	subject	subject

MON. /

TUES. /

WED. /

THURS. /

FRI. /

subject	subject	subject	subject

WEEK

subject	subject	subject

MON.
/

TUES.
/

WED.
/

THURS.
/

FRI.
/

subject	subject	subject	subject

WEEK

subject	subject	subject

MON.
/

TUES.
/

WED.
/

THURS.
/

FRI.
/

subject	subject	subject	subject

WEEK

subject	subject	subject

MON.
/

TUES.
/

WED.
/

THURS.
/

FRI.
/

subject	subject	subject	subject

WEEK

subject	subject	subject

MON.
/

TUES.
/

WED.
/

THURS.
/

FRI.
/

subject	subject	subject	subject

WEEK

subject	subject	subject

MON. /

TUES. /

WED. /

THURS. /

FRI. /

subject	subject	subject	subject

WEEK#

subject	subject	subject

MON.
/

TUES.
/

WED.
/

THURS.
/

FRI.
/

subject	subject	subject	subject

WEEK

subject	subject	subject

MON.
/

subject	subject	subject

TUES.
/

WED.
/

THURS.
/

FRI.
/

subject	subject	subject	subject

WEEK

subject	subject	subject

MON.
/

TUES.
/

WED.
/

THURS.
/

FRI.
/

subject	subject	subject	subject

WEEK

subject	subject	subject

MON. /

TUES. /

WED. /

THURS. /

FRI. /

subject	subject	subject	subject

WEEK

subject	subject	subject

MON.
/

TUES.
/

WED.
/

THURS.
/

FRI.
/

subject	subject	subject	subject

WEEK

subject	subject	subject

MON.
/

TUES.
/

WED.
/

THURS.
/

FRI.
/

subject	subject	subject	subject

WEEK

subject	subject	subject

MON.
/

TUES.
/

WED.
/

THURS.
/

FRI.
/

subject	subject	subject	subject

WEEK

subject	subject	subject

MON.
/

TUES.
/

WED.
/

THURS.
/

FRI.
/

subject	subject	subject	subject

WEEK

subject	subject	subject

MON.
/

TUES.
/

WED.
/

THURS.
/

FRI.
/

subject	subject	subject	subject

WEEK

subject	subject	subject

MON.
/

TUES.
/

WED.
/

THURS.
/

FRI.
/

subject	subject	subject	subject

WEEK

subject	subject	subject

MON.
/

TUES.
/

WED.
/

THURS.
/

FRI.
/

subject	subject	subject	subject

CHECKLIST

Name

CHECKLIST

Name

PSST! CUT THIS SECTION OFF SO YOU ONLY HAVE TO WRITE YOUR CLASS LIST ONCE.

CHECKLIST

Name

CHECKLIST

Name

CHECKLIST

Name

CHECKLIST

Name